A Little Princess

Frances Hodgson Burnett

Text adaptation by Jennifer Bassett
Illustrated by Bob Doucet

Original Bookworms Series Editor:
Jennifer Bassett

OXFORD
UNIVERSITY PRESS

Activities

Before reading

Sara Crewe is a very rich little girl. She first comes to England when she is seven, and her father takes her to Miss Minchin's school in London. Then he goes back to his work in India. Sara is sad at first, but she soon makes lots of friends at her new school. But then something terrible happens in India and Sara's life changes. . .

1 **Read the introduction to the story. Then tick the correct boxes.**

	Yes	No
1 Sara Crewe is rich.	✓	☐
2 Sara comes to England for a holiday.	☐	☐
3 Miss Minchin likes Sara because her father is kind.	☐	☐
4 Sara is happy when her father leaves.	☐	☐
5 Sara is a princess.	☐	☐

2 **What do you think happens that is terrible? Tick the boxes.**

	Yes	No
1 Mr Crewe dies.	☐	☐
2 Mr Crewe goes to prison.	☐	☐
3 Mr Crewe loses all his money.	☐	☐
4 Sara is poor, hungry and sad all her life.	☐	☐
5 Sara goes back to India.	☐	☐

CHAPTER 1 School in England

One cold winter day a little girl and her father arrived in London. Sara Crewe was seven years old, and she had long dark hair and green eyes. She sat in the cab next to her father and looked out of the window at the tall houses and the dark sky.

'What are you thinking about, Sara?' Mr Crewe asked. 'You are very quiet.'

'I'm thinking about our house in India,' said Sara. 'And the hot sun and the blue sky. I don't think I like England very much, Father.'

cab a taxi or a carriage pulled by horses

'Yes, it's very different from India,' her father said. 'But you must go to school in London, and I must go back to India and work.'

'Yes, Father, I know,' said Sara. 'But I want to be with you. Please come to school with me! I can help you with your lessons.'

Mr Crewe smiled, but he was not happy. He loved his little Sara very much, and he did not want to be without her. Sara's mother was dead, and Sara was his only child. Father and daughter were very good friends.

Soon they arrived at Miss Minchin's School for Girls and went into the big house.

Miss Minchin was a tall woman in a black dress. She looked at Sara, and then gave a very big smile.

'What a beautiful child!' she said to Mr Crewe.

Sara stood quietly and watched Miss Minchin. 'Why does she say that?' she thought. 'I am not beautiful, so why does she say it?'

Sara was not beautiful, but her father was rich. And Miss Minchin liked girls with rich fathers, because it was good for the school (and good for Miss Minchin, too).

'Sara is a good girl,' Mr Crewe said to Miss Minchin. 'Her mother was French, so she speaks French well. She loves books, and she reads all the time. But she must play with the other girls and make new friends, too.'

'Of course,' said Miss Minchin. She smiled again. 'Sara is going to be very happy here, Mr Crewe.'

Mr Crewe stayed in London for a week. He and Sara went to the shops, and he bought many beautiful, expensive dresses for his daughter. He bought books, and flowers for her room, and a big doll with beautiful dresses, too.

without not with

rich with lots of money

buy (past **bought**) to give money for something

Miss Minchin smiled, but she said to her sister Amelia: 'All that money on dresses for a child of seven! She looks like a little princess, not a schoolgirl!'

*   *   *

When Mr Crewe left London, he was very sad. Sara was very sad too, but she did not cry. She sat in her room and thought about her father on the ship back to India.

princess the daughter of a king or queen

leave (past left) to go away from someone or something

ship a big boat

'Father wants me to be happy,' she said to her new doll. 'I love him very much and I want to be a good daughter, so I must be happy.'

It was a very big and very beautiful doll, but of course it could not answer.

Sara soon made new friends in the school. Some little rich girls are not very nice – they think they are important because they have money and lots of expensive things. But Sara was different. She liked beautiful dresses and dolls, but she was more interested in people and books, and telling stories.

She was very good at telling stories. She was a clever child, and the other girls loved to listen to her. The stories were all about kings and queens and princesses and wonderful countries across the sea.

'How do you think of all those things?' asked her best friend, Ermengarde.

'I have all these pictures in my head,' said Sara. 'So it's easy to tell stories about them.'

Poor Ermengarde was not clever. She could never remember any of her school lessons, and Miss Minchin was always angry with her.

Sara often helped Ermengarde with her lessons.

'Listen, Ermie,' she said. 'You remember that French king, Louis the Sixteenth? Well, this is a story about him. One day in 1792 ...'

clever quick-thinking, able to learn and do things well

remember to think about something you know

6

And so Ermengarde learnt her lessons with Sara's stories, and she loved her friend very much. But not everybody was Sara's friend. Lavinia was an older girl. Before Sara came, Lavinia was the richest and the most important girl in the school. But Sara's father was richer than Lavinia's father. So now Sara was more important than Lavinia, and Lavinia did not like that.

'Oh, Sara is *so* clever!' Lavinia sometimes said. 'Sara is *so* good at French! Her dresses are *so* beautiful, and she can sing *so* well! And she is *so* rich! Of course Miss Minchin likes her best!'

Sara did not answer when Lavinia said these things. Sometimes it was not easy, but Sara was a kind, friendly girl, and she did not like to be angry with anyone.

Activities

1 Complete the sentences with these words.

| clever | expensive | lessons | like | princess | sad | rich | richer |

1 Miss Minchin liked Sara because her father was ___rich___ .

2 Mr Crewe bought many _expensive_ things for his daughter.

3 Miss Minchin thought Sara looked like a little _princess_ .

4 When Mr Crewe left London, Sara was very _sad_ .

5 Sara's friend Ermengarde was not _clever_ , so Sara helped her

with her school _lessons_ .

6 Sara's father was _richer_ than Lavinia's father, and because

of that, Lavinia did not _like_ Sara.

2 Who said this? Write the names.

| Miss Minchin | Ermengarde | Lavinia | Sara | Mr Crewe |

1 'I don't think I like England very much.' ___Sara___

2 'I must go back to India and work.' _Mr Crewe_

3 'All that money on dresses!' _____

4 'How do you think of all those things?' _Erme_

5 'Sara is rich! Of course Miss Minchin likes her best!' _____

3 Rewrite these words from Chapter 1. Then complete each sentence with one word.

1 ynagr   a _ngry_

2 eretintsed   i _interested_

3 pinttroma   i _____

4 ufeabitul   b _beautiful_

5 oogd   g _good_

6 erermemb   r _remember_

7 hicr   r _rich_

a 'What a _____ child!' Miss Minchin said to Mr Crewe.

b Sara did not like to be _____ angry _____ with anyone.

c Miss Minchin liked girls with _____ fathers.

d Sara was _____ in people and books, and telling stories.

e 'I want to be a _____ daughter,' thinks Sara.

f Some rich children think they are _____ because they have got a lot of money.

g Ermengarde could never _____ her lessons.

Chapter 2 **The diamond mines**

mine place where people look for diamonds under the ground

diamond a very expensive stone that usually has no colour

And so three years went by. Sara's father wrote to her every week, and Sara wrote lots of letters back to him. One day a very exciting letter arrived. Everybody in the school talked about it for days.

'My friend,' wrote Mr Crewe, 'has some mines in northern India, and a month ago his workers found diamonds there. There are thousands of diamonds in these mines, but it is expensive work to get them out. My friend needs my help. So, Little Missus' (this was Mr Crewe's special name for Sara), 'I am putting all my money into my friend's diamond mines, and one day you and I are going to be very rich ...'

Sara was not interested in money, but a story about diamond mines in India was exciting. Everybody was very happy for Sara, but not Lavinia, of course.

'Huh!' she said. 'My mother's got a diamond. Lots of people have got diamonds. What's so interesting about diamond mines?'

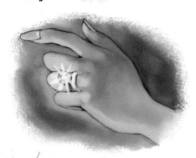

'But there are thousands of diamonds in these mines,' said Ermengarde. 'Maybe millions of them!'

Lavinia laughed. 'Is Sara going to wear diamonds in her hair at breakfast, then? Or is it "Princess Sara" now?'

Sara's face went red. She looked at Lavinia angrily, but said quietly, 'Some people call me "princess". I know that. But princesses don't get angry or say unkind things, so I'm not going to say anything to you, Lavinia.'

'To me, you *are* a princess,' Ermengarde said to Sara later. 'And you always look like a princess in your beautiful dresses.'

* * *

Sara was a princess to another girl, too. This was Becky. She was a servant in Miss Minchin's school, and she was only fourteen years old, but she worked all day and sometimes half the night. She carried things upstairs and downstairs, she cleaned the floors, she made the fires, and she was always tired and hungry and dirty. She and Sara had very different lives.

But one day Sara came into her bedroom, and there was Becky, sleeping in a chair.

'Oh, you poor thing!' Sara said.

millions many thousands

servant a person who works for someone rich

fire something that burns and makes the room hot

Then Becky opened her eyes and saw Sara. She got up at once. 'Oh, Miss!' she said. 'I'm very sorry, Miss! I just sat down for a minute and —'

'Don't be scared,' said Sara. She gave Becky a friendly smile. 'You were tired. That's all.'

'Are you — are you going to tell Miss Minchin?' asked Becky. She began to go to the door.

'Of course not,' said Sara. 'Please don't run away. Sit down again for a minute. You look very tired.'

'Oh, Miss, I can't!' Becky said. 'You're very kind, Miss, but Miss Minchin —'

'Please,' said Sara. She took Becky's hand. 'You're only a little girl, like me. Let's be friends.'

And so Becky sat down again, and soon she and Sara were friends.

Nobody knew about this, of course. Rich little girls at Miss Minchin's school did not make friends with servant-girls, and it was a wonderful thing for Becky. Every day she and Sara met in Sara's bedroom, just for five or ten minutes. Becky was always hungry, and Sara bought nice things for her to eat. They sat and talked, and sometimes Sara told Becky some of her stories. Becky loved that.

party a fun, happy time with food and games

'Oh, Miss,' she said. 'You tell stories so beautifully! Sometimes I like your stories better than things to eat.'

And after those visits to Sara's room, Becky always felt better – not so tired, and not so hungry.

*   *   *

Some months later Sara had her eleventh birthday. Lessons stopped for the afternoon and there was a big party for all the girls in the school.

'This party is expensive for us,' Miss Minchin said to her sister Amelia. 'But it looks good for the school.'

That afternoon there was a visitor to the school — Miss Minchin's lawyer. He went with Miss Minchin into her office and they closed the door. In the schoolroom next door there was a lot of noise from Sara's party. Everybody in there was very happy.

But in the office Miss Minchin was not happy. She looked at the lawyer angrily. 'What are you saying? Mr Crewe has no money? What about the diamond mines?'

'There are *no* diamond mines,' said the lawyer. 'Well, there are mines, but there are no diamonds in them.'

'But Mr Crewe's good friend —' began Miss Minchin.

'Mr Crewe's good friend,' said the lawyer, 'ran away with all Mr Crewe's money. Ralph Crewe was ill with a fever, and when he heard about this, he got worse. A week later he was dead.'

'Dead!' cried Miss Minchin. 'But what about his daughter Sara? And this expensive birthday party?'

'Sara Crewe has no money,' said the lawyer. 'Not a penny in the world, Miss Minchin. Not a penny.'

'She must leave my school at once,' Miss Minchin said angrily. 'She must go this afternoon!'

'Where?' said the lawyer. 'Out into the streets? An eleven-year-old girl? That's not going to look very good for your school, Miss Minchin.'

Miss Minchin's face went red.

'You can't put her out in the streets,' said the lawyer. He stood up. 'But maybe she can work for you.'

The lawyer left, and Miss Minchin called her sister Amelia. 'Bring Sara Crewe here at once,' she said.

Two minutes later Sara, in her beautiful blue party dress, stood in front of Miss Minchin.

'Have you got a black dress, Sara?' Miss Minchin said coldly.

'Yes, Miss Minchin,' said Sara. 'But it's very old.'

'Go and put it on at once,' said Miss Minchin. 'Your father is dead. There were no diamond mines, and your father's friend ran away with all his money. You have nothing. Not a penny. But I am going to be very kind to you. You can stay in my house, but now you must be a servant and work for your bread. You can sleep in a servant's room upstairs, next to Becky's room.'

fever when you
are ill with a very
hot head and body

penny a small
coin, money

Activities

1 Who said or wrote this, and who to?

| Ermengarde | Sara | Becky | Miss Minchin | Ralph Crewe | the lawyer |

1 'My friend has some mines in northern India.'
   Ralph Crewe wrote this to Sara.

2 'To me, you are a princess.'
   _____

3 'Sit down again for a minute. You look very tired.'
   _____

4 'Sometimes I like your stories better than things to eat.'
   _____

5 'Mr Crewe's good friend ran away with all Mr Crewe's money.'
   _____

6 'She must leave my school at once.'
   _____

7 '. . . you must be a servant and work for your bread.'
   _____

2 Circle the odd-one-out.

1 week / year / day / (story) / month

2 beautiful / bad / exciting / wonderful / good

3 blue / black / white / big / green

4 sister / father / friend / daughter / mother

5 talk / speak / say / laugh / write

3 **The lawyer is telling someone about Sara. Choose the correct words.**

'Sara Crewe? Oh yes, she came to Miss Minchin's school over three **months /
years** ago. Her father was very **rich / kind**. Then he had a serious **accident /
illness** and he died. Now Sara has no **money / friends**. Miss Minchin wanted her
to **leave / stay** and told her she must work as a **servant / cook**.'

4 **Find words in the word snake to complete the sentences.**

1 The workers found thousands of ____diamonds____ in the mines.
2 Becky was a _____ in Miss Minchin's school.
3 Becky cleaned floors and made _____ .
4 On Sara's birthday, there was a big _____ .
5 The _____ told Miss Minchin there were no diamonds.
6 Ralph Crewe died from a _____ .

5 **Write the names.**

| Miss Minchin | Ermengarde | Lavinia | ~~Becky~~ |

____Becky____   _____   _____   _____

Before you read Chapter 3, can you guess the answer to this question?

Are any of these people going to be kind to Sara? _____

Chapter 3 **The new servant-girl**

attic a small
room under the
roof of a house
where servants
had their rooms

late at the end of
the day

whisper to speak
very quietly

That evening, in the little attic room, Sara sat on the bed in her old black dress. She did not cry, but her face was white and she did not speak for hours.

Late at night the door opened quietly, and Becky looked in. Her eyes were red from crying. 'Oh, Miss,' she said. 'All the servants are talking about it. I'm so sorry — so sorry!' She looked at Sara's white face, and began to cry again. Then she ran to Sara and took her hand.

At last Sara slowly turned her head and looked at Becky. 'Oh, Becky,' she said. And that was all.

That first night in the attic was very long. Sara did not sleep. 'Father is dead,' she whispered, again and again. 'Father is dead. I'm never going to see him again.'

The next morning Sara's new life started. She learnt to clean floors and to make fires. She ran upstairs and downstairs, and she worked in the kitchen.

The cook was a big woman with a red, angry face. 'So,' she said, 'the little rich girl with the diamond mines is now a servant, eh?' She looked at Sara. 'Now, I'm making apple pies this morning. Run down to the shops and get me some apples. And be quick!'

So Sara ran to the shops, and carried a big bag of apples back to the house. Then she cleaned the kitchen floor and carried hot water up to all the bedrooms.

She worked every day, from early in the morning to late at night. She helped in the school, too.

'You speak French well,' Miss Minchin said to her coldly. 'So you can teach French to the younger children. But you're only a servant. Don't forget that.'

The first months of Sara's new life were very hard. She was always tired and hungry, but she never cried. At night, in her little attic, she thought about her father, dead in India all those miles away.

'I must be brave,' she said. 'Father always wanted me to be brave. And I've got a bed to sleep in, and something to eat every day. Lots of people haven't got that.'

At first Sara's only friend was Becky. Every day Becky came into Sara's room. They did not talk much, but it helped Sara a lot to see Becky's friendly, smiling face.

The girls in the school were sorry for Sara, but Sara was a servant now, and they could not be friendly with a servant. Lavinia, of course, was happy. 'I never liked Sara Crewe,' she told her friends. 'And I was right about the diamonds – there weren't any!'

Ermengarde was very unhappy. When she saw Sara in

early at the start of the day

teach to give lessons to other people

forget not to remember something

brave not crying or asking for help when you are very sad

be sorry for to be unhappy about

19

the school, Sara walked past her and did not speak. Poor Ermengarde loved Sara and wanted to be friendly, but she was not clever and she did not understand.

One morning, very early, she got out of bed quietly, went upstairs to the attic, and opened Sara's door.

'Ermengarde!' Sara said. 'What are you doing here?'

Ermengarde started to cry. 'Oh, Sara, please tell me. What *is* the matter? Why don't you like me now?'

'I *do* like you,' Sara said. 'Of course I do. But, you see, everything is different now. Miss Minchin doesn't want me to talk to the girls. Most of them don't want to talk to me. And I thought, maybe, you didn't want to ...'

'But I'm your *friend*!' cried Ermengarde. 'I'm *always* going to be your friend – and *nobody* can stop me!'

Sara took Ermengarde's hands. She suddenly felt very happy. Maybe she cried a little, too.

There was only one chair, so the two friends sat on the bed. Ermengarde looked round the attic. 'Oh, Sara, how can you live in this room? It's so cold and – and dirty.'

'It's not so bad,' said Sara. 'And I've got lots of friends. There's Becky in the next room, and – come and see.'

She put the table under the window, and then she and Ermengarde stood on it and looked out of the window, over the roofs of the houses. In her pocket Sara had some small pieces of bread. She put her hand out of the window, with the bread on it. 'Watch,' she said.

After a minute a little brown bird flew down to Sara's hand and started to eat the bread. Then a second bird came, and a third, and a fourth.

'Oh Sara, how wonderful!' said Ermengarde.

'They know I'm their friend,' said Sara, 'so they're not afraid of me.'

roof the top of a house

Ermengarde looked across the roof to the next attic window. 'Who lives in that house?' she asked.

'Nobody,' said Sara sadly. 'So I never see anybody at that window, and I can only talk to the birds.'

* * *

But one night, two or three weeks later, Becky came into Sara's room. She was very excited.

'Oooh, Miss!' she said. 'An Indian gentleman is moving into the house next door. Well, he's English, but he lived in India for years and years. And now he's going to live next door. He's very rich, and he's ill. Something bad happened to him, but I don't know what.'

Sara laughed. 'How do you know all this?' she said.

'Well, Miss, you know the Carmichael family across the street?' Becky said. 'I'm friendly with their kitchen-girl, and she told me. Mr Carmichael is the Indian gentleman's lawyer, so they know all about him.'

gentleman a man from a good family, who is sometimes rich

move into to take all your things and live in a different place

next door the nearest house to your house

Activities

1 Are these sentences true (T) or false (F)? Correct the false sentences.

never

1 Sara ~~often~~ cried in the first months of her new life. $\boxed{F}$

2 She worked from early in the morning to late at night. ☐

3 One morning Lavinia came up to her attic room. ☐

4 Sara was very sad when Ermengarde came to see her. ☐

5 Sara never saw anybody at the next attic window. ☐

6 Then the Carmichael family came to live next door. ☐

2 Complete the sentences with the correct name.

Becky Sara Lavinia ~~The cook~~ Ermengarde Miss Minchin

1 _____The cook_____ was a big woman who worked in the kitchen.

2 _____ taught French to the younger children.

3 _____ was unhappy without her friend and visited her in her attic room.

4 _____ had some news about a gentleman who was going to live next door.

5 _____ was happy that Sara wasn't important in the school any more.

6 _____ told Sara never to forget she was a servant.

3 **Complete the sentences and write the words in the crossword.**

1 Sara's friend ___Ermengarde___ visited her early one morning.

2 Sara showed Ermengarde how she could look out of her _____.

3 Miss Minchin asked Sara to teach _____ to the younger children in the school.

4 As a servant-girl, Sara had to _____ very hard.

5 Sara fed pieces of _____ to the brown birds.

6 Mr Carmichael is the Indian gentleman's _____.

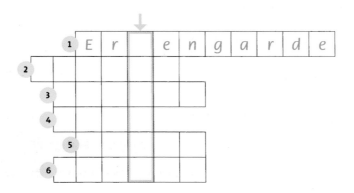

1 E | r | | e | n | g | a | r | d | e

4 **Read the word (↓) and write the name of the animal Sara sees in the next chapter.**

_m_ _____

Chapter 4 Ram Dass and the monkey

Every morning, when Sara gave the birds their bread, she looked across to the attic window next door. But nobody opened it. Nobody called out 'Good morning!' across the roof, or gave Sara a friendly smile.

'Perhaps the Indian gentleman's servants all sleep downstairs,' she thought sadly.

Her life was very lonely now. She saw Becky every day, of course, but they did not have much time for talking. The cook and the other servants were not friendly. Sometimes, at night, Ermengarde came up to Sara's room, but it was not easy for her to come often.

Then one evening, Sara was in her attic when she heard a noise on the roof. She looked up – and there at the open window was a small monkey.

'Oh, you dear little thing!' cried Sara.

At once, the monkey jumped down and started to run round the room. Sara laughed. She got up on the table and looked out of her window, and at the next window she saw a face – the smiling face of an Indian lascar.

'Oh,' cried Sara, 'have you got a monkey? He's in my room.'

The lascar's name was Ram Dass, and yes, it was his monkey. He gave Sara a big smile.

'I'm very sorry,' he said. 'Can I come and get him?'

'Oh yes, please,' said Sara. 'I think he's scared of me. And he runs so fast! But can you get across the roof?'

Yes, Ram Dass could, and a minute later he was at Sara's window. Soon the monkey jumped into his arms, and Ram Dass thanked Sara again and again. Then he went away, across the roof, back into the house next door.

Sara went to the shops five or six times a day, and when she walked past the house next door, she thought about the Indian gentleman. She was sorry for him. He had no wife or family, and the doctor visited the house every day. Mr Carmichael the lawyer visited too, and sometimes the Carmichael children went with him.

Sara was happy about that. 'It's nice to see friendly faces when you are ill,' she thought.

The Indian gentleman thought that, too. He liked children very much, but he was a very unhappy man. Mr Carmichael was his friend, and he talked to him a lot. But they talked about only one thing.

jump to move quickly from one place to another place

lascar an Indian sailor

doctor a person who helps people get better

ill not well

take care of to
give someone love,
a home and food

half (plural
halves) two parts

nearly almost

'I must find the child,' said the Indian gentleman (his name was Mr Carrisford). 'I must find her and take care of her. But where is she? Here I am, with all this money from the diamond mines – and half of it is Ralph Crewe's money. Oh, Carmichael, why did I leave my friend and run away when things looked bad? Why?'

'You ran away because you were ill with a fever,' said Mr Carmichael. 'It nearly killed you, remember?'

'And it *did* kill poor Ralph,' said Mr Carrisford. 'He put all his money into the mines because I was his friend. But at first we didn't find any diamonds, and all Ralph's money was gone. I was too afraid to tell him, so I ran away. And later, when we *did* find diamonds, Ralph was dead.' He laughed, angrily. 'What a brave friend I was!'

'It's not easy to be brave,' Mr Carmichael said quietly, 'when you're ill with a fever.'

Mr Carrisford looked into the fire. 'Ram Dass tells me,'

he said, 'about a little servant-girl next door. The monkey ran away, and Ram Dass went across the roof to get him from her room. The poor child sleeps in a cold, dirty attic, and works about sixteen hours a day. Is Ralph's daughter living like that? I can't stop thinking about it.'

'We're going to find her one day,' said Mr Carmichael.

'But how?' said Mr Carrisford. He put his head in his hands. 'I've never seen her. I don't know her name! Ralph always called her his "Little Missus". We talked all the time about the mines. He never told me the name of her school. Her mother was French, so did he take her to a school in France? Or was it in England?'

'Well, we know there was a child at a school in Paris,' said Mr Carmichael, 'with the name of Carew or Crewe. Her father died suddenly, and a Russian family took her away with them, because she was a friend of their daughter. Perhaps this girl is Ralph Crewe's child. Next week I'm going to Moscow to look for her.'

'I want to go with you, but I'm not well,' said Mr Carrisford. 'I must find her, Carmichael. I must. Every night, I dream. I see Ralph Crewe's face, and he says: "Tom, Tom, where is my Little Missus?" And I have no answer for him.' Mr Carrisford took his friend's hand. 'Help me to find her. Help me.'

*   *   *

Winter came, with its short, dark days, and the attic rooms were very cold. There were no fires for servant-girls, and often Sara and Becky could not sleep because of the cold. Sara was taller now, and her old black dress was very short. Her shoes were old, and she had no warm coat for the winter weather. She was thin, too. She did not get very much to eat, and she was always hungry.

suddenly quickly, with no one expecting it

thin not fat

She carried big bags of shopping through the rain and the snow. One day she found a sixpence in the snow, and she bought some hot bread with it. Then she saw a child by the door of the shop. The child had no shoes and no coat, and her thin face was blue with cold.

'She is hungrier than I am,' thought Sara. And she gave her hot bread to the child.

When she got back to the school, Miss Minchin was angry. 'Cook is waiting for you, Sara. Why are you late?'

'I can't walk quickly through the snow,' said Sara. 'My shoes are old, Miss Minchin, and my feet get very cold.'

Miss Minchin did not like to hear this. 'Don't speak to me like that!' she said. 'I am kind to you, I'm giving you a home, but you never say "thank you" to me.'

Sara looked at her. 'You are *not* kind,' she said quietly. 'And this is *not* a home.'

'Go to your room at once!' said Miss Minchin.

On the stairs Sara met Lavinia. Lavinia looked at her and gave a little laugh. 'Oh, here's Princess Sara,' she said, 'in her old dress and her dirty shoes!'

In the attic, Sara sat down on the chair by her table.

'I must be brave,' she whispered. 'A princess is always brave, so I must be, too. But it's not easy.' She put her head down on her arms. 'Oh, Father, do you remember your Little Missus? Can you see me now?'

And in the house next door Mr Carrisford sat by a warm fire. Moscow is a long way from London, and he could only wait, but he thought about Ralph Crewe's child every day. He thought about other children, too.

'Ram Dass,' he said. 'How is that poor little servant-girl next door? Can we do something for her?'

'I see her in the street every day,' said Ram Dass. 'In the rain, in the snow. She looks thin and hungry. But we can help her. I can easily get in through her attic window. Listen ...' And he talked for some minutes.

Mr Carrisford smiled. 'Yes,' he said to Ram Dass. 'Yes, I like it. Let's do it.'

think (*past thought*) to have an idea about something

street road

29

Activities

1 What do they say? Complete the sentences.

> Let's help the little girl next door!

> Yes, can I come and get him?

> I must find the child!

> I have an idea what we can do!

> I'm going to Moscow to look for her.

> Yes, but can you get across the roof?

> I've got him now – thank you, thank you!

> ~~Have you got a monkey?~~

1 _'Have you got a monkey?'_ Sara asked Ram Dass.

2 _____ answered Ram Dass.

3 _____ Sara asked.

4 _____ said Ram Dass to Sara.

5 _____ Mr Carrisford said to his lawyer.

6 _____ Mr Carmichael said to Mr Carrisford.

7 _____ Mr Carrisford said to Ram Dass.

8 _____ Ram Dass said to Mr Carrisford.

2 Answer these questions.

Why

1 ... did Ram Dass come across the roof to Sara's room?
   Because he followed the monkey.

2 ... was Sara sorry for the Indian gentleman?

3 ... did Mr Carrisford want to find Ralph Crewe's child?

4 ... did Mr Carrisford run away from Ralph in India?

5 ... was Mr Carrisford sorry for the little servant-girl next door?

6 ... did Mr Carmichael go to Moscow?

7 ... did Sara give her bread to a child in the street?

8 ... was Sara very unhappy that night?

3 What do you think happens next? Tick the boxes.

1 Ram Dass goes to Sara's attic, but Sara doesn't see him. ☐
2 Ram Dass leaves some money for Sara in her room. ☐
3 Sara talks to Ram Dass and tells him her name. ☐
4 Ram Dass tells Mr Carrisford that Sara is Ralph Crewe's daughter. ☐
5 The monkey runs away again to Sara's room. ☐

Chapter 5 'Am I dreaming?'

One night, a week later, Ermengarde got out of bed quietly and went upstairs to the attic. Sara was not there, so Ermengarde sat on the bed and waited. At ten o'clock Sara came slowly up the stairs and into the room.

Ermengarde looked at her. 'Oh, Sara!' she cried. 'Are you ill? Your face is white, and you look so tired!'

'It was a hard day, Ermie,' said Sara. She sat down. 'Miss Minchin was angry with Cook. Then Cook was angry with us. Becky and I had no dinner and no tea.'

'Does that happen often?' said Ermengarde unhappily. 'You never told me. Are you – are you hungry now?'

Sara looked at her. 'Yes,' she whispered. 'Yes, I am. I would like to eat that table. I would like to eat *you*.'

Ermengarde jumped up. 'Sara,' she cried. 'I had a box of things from home today. There's a big cake in it. I'm going to get it now! You and Becky can eat it all!'

Soon, Ermengarde was back. The three girls sat on Sara's bed, and there were some happy smiles when Ermengarde opened her box and took out the cake.

'Oh, Miss, look at that!' said Becky.

'You are *kind*, Ermie,' said Sara. She laughed. 'When things are very bad, something nice always happens. Here we are, having a party!'

Ermengarde gave Sara and Becky some cake,

and they started to eat. Suddenly, they stopped. There
was a noise of feet on the stairs. They listened.

'Oh no!' whispered Becky. 'It's – it's Miss Minchin!'

'Yes,' said Sara. Her face was white again.

Then the door opened and Miss Minchin came in.

'So, Lavinia was right,' she said angrily. 'Tea with Princess
Sara! Becky, get back to your attic at once!'

'Oh, please, Miss Minchin!' cried Ermengarde. 'It was my
cake, from home. We're only having a party.'

blanket warm
cover for your bed

'Go back to your room, Ermengarde,' Miss Minchin said coldly, 'and take these things with you. And tomorrow' – she looked at Sara – 'there's no breakfast, no dinner and no tea for you. Remember that!'

* * *

Soon the attic rooms were quiet again. Tired and hungry, the two servant-girls went to sleep. But after an hour or two Sara opened her eyes. Was it a noise from the window perhaps?

'Something is *different*,' Sara whispered. 'What is it?' She sat up in bed and looked round the room. She looked again and again, and her eyes were very big.

The room *was* different – very different. There was a wonderful hot fire. There were new, warm blankets on her bed, and beautiful pictures on the walls.

Sara slowly got out of bed. 'Am I dreaming?' she said. 'Where did all these things come from?' She put out her hand to the fire. 'No, it's not a dream. The fire is hot — I can feel it. And oh! Look at the table!'

There was a red cloth on the table, and cups and plates. There was hot tea, and wonderful things to eat — hot meat pies and sandwiches and cake, oranges and apples.

Sara ran to Becky's room. 'Becky,' she whispered. 'Come quickly. Come and look.'

When Becky saw the room, she could not speak at first. Then she said, 'Oh, Miss! What is it? How did all these things get here?'

'I don't know,' said Sara. 'At first I thought it was a dream, but it isn't. Look — these pies are hot. Let's eat them. Hot meat pies aren't a dream!'

They sat down by the fire, and ate and drank.

'Oh, those pies were good, Miss!' Becky said. 'And the tea and the cake. I don't understand it, but I like it!'

Sara looked round the room. 'Oh, Becky, look! There are some books, too. I didn't see them before.'

She ran to look at them, and opened the top book. 'There's some writing here! Listen. It says, "To the little girl in the attic. From a friend." Oh, Becky!' Sara closed the book and looked up. 'I've got a friend, Becky,' she said slowly. 'Someone is my friend.'

* * *

The next morning Becky met Sara in the kitchen.

'Oh, Miss,' she whispered. 'Was it all a dream last night? The meat pies and the fire and everything?'

'No, it wasn't a dream,' Sara whispered back. 'I ate some cold meat pie for breakfast. And the fire was still warm!'

cloth cover for the table

meat pie food made with meat and pastry

Becky laughed happily. 'Oh my! Oh my!' she said.

Miss Minchin could not understand it. When Sara came into the schoolroom, she looked happy and well. Miss Minchin wanted to see a white, unhappy face, and eyes red from crying. 'How can that child smile?' she thought angrily. But of course, she did not know about the hot meat pies.

* * *

Every evening, when Sara went up to bed, she found new things in the attic. There were more warm blankets for her and for Becky. There were pictures on the walls; there were books, new shoes and a winter coat. And best of all, there was always a fire, and a wonderful hot dinner on the table.

'But where does it all come from?' Becky said one night when they sat by the fire. 'Who does it, Miss?'

'A friend does it,' Sara said. 'A kind, wonderful friend. But he doesn't want us to know his name.'

They began to look at one of the new books, and then Becky looked up.

'Oh, Miss,' she whispered. 'There's something at the window. What is it?'

Sara got up to look. 'It's the monkey!' she said. 'The monkey from next door.' She opened the window and the monkey jumped down into her arms. 'Oh, you poor little thing,' Sara said. 'You're so cold!'

Becky was very interested. 'I've never seen a monkey before,' she said. 'He's not very beautiful, Miss! What are you going to do with him?'

'It's very late now,' said Sara. 'He can stay in my room tonight and I can take him to his home in the morning.'

Activities

1 How did Miss Minchin find out about Ermengarde's cake and the tea party in the attic? Put her conversation with Lavinia in the correct order, and write in the speakers' names.

a _____ 'She's upstairs, in the attic.' ☐

b _____ 'Yes, Lavinia, what is it?' ☐

c _____ 'A big cake. She said Sara was hungry.' ☐

d _____ 'Having tea with—! How do you know this, Lavinia?' ☐

e ___*Lavinia*___ 'Oh, Miss Minchin. I have something to tell you!' ☐1

f _____ 'A box? What was in it?' ☐

g _____ 'She's having tea with Princess Sara.' ☐

h _____ 'Of course she isn't hungry! Right. I'm going upstairs at once. You were right to tell me this, Lavinia. You can go back to bed now.' ☐

i _____ 'I saw her on the stairs, with a big box.' ☐

j _____ 'But it's after ten o'clock! Where is she?' ☐

k _____ 'What's she doing up there?' ☐

l _____ 'Ermengarde isn't in her bed, Miss Minchin.' ☐

2 Correct the underlined words in these sentences.

1 Sara was hungry because she didn't have any <u>digger</u>. ___*dinner*___

2 When Sara woke up there were warm <u>brackets</u> on her bed. _____

3 There was a red <u>cloak</u> on the table. _____

4 Sara had some cold <u>meal tie</u> for breakfast. _____

5 Sara's kind friend didn't want her to know his <u>game</u>. _____

3 Match the two halves of the sentences.

1 One night Ermengarde took a cake to Sara's room, . . .

2 Later that night Sara found some wonderful things in her room, . . .

3 Every evening after that, when Sara went to bed, . . .

4 Miss Minchin couldn't understand why . . .

5 Sara knew that she had a kind, wonderful friend, . . .

6 Then the monkey came to Sara's room one night, . . .

a and ran to tell Becky.

b and Sara took him back to the Indian gentleman's house.

c but Miss Minchin came up and stopped the party.

d but she did not know his name.

e there were new things in the attic for her and for Becky.

f Sara was looking happy and well.

4 What do you think happens at the end of the story? Tick the boxes.

	Yes	No
1 Sara tells Mr Carrisford about her father's death.	☐	☐
2 Sara goes to live with Mr Carrisford.	☐	☐
3 Lavinia becomes Sara's maid.	☐	☐
4 Sara never sees Ermengarde again.	☐	☐
5 Sara discovers she is rich after all.	☐	☐

Chapter 6 **Lost and found**

The next morning, the first visitor to the house next door was Mr Carmichael, back from Russia. But when he came into the house, his face was sad. Mr Carrisford knew the answer at once.

'You didn't find her,' he said.

'I found her,' Mr Carmichael said. 'But it was the wrong girl. Her name is Emily Carew, and she's much younger than Ralph Crewe's daughter. I'm very sorry.'

'We must start again,' said Mr Carrisford unhappily. 'But where? It's two years now. Two years!'

'Well, she isn't at a school in Paris. We know that,' Mr Carmichael said. 'Let's look at schools in England now.'

'Yes,' said Mr Carrisford. 'Yes, we can start in London. There's a school next door, Carmichael.'

At that moment Ram Dass came quietly into the room.

'The little servant-girl from the attic is here,' he said to Mr Carrisford. 'With the monkey. He ran away again last night to her room. Would you like to see her?'

'Yes,' said Mr Carrisford. 'Yes, I would. Bring her in.'

And so Sara came into the room and stood in front of the Indian gentleman. She smiled at him.

'Your monkey came to my room last night,' she said, 'and I took him in because it was so cold.'

Mr Carrisford watched her face with interest. 'That was kind of you,' he said.

Sara looked at Ram Dass by the door. 'Do you want me to give him to the lascar?' she asked.

'How do you know he is a lascar?' said Mr Carrisford.

'Oh, I know lascars,' Sara said. 'I was born in India.'

Mr Carrisford sat up suddenly. 'In India?' he said. 'But

you're a servant at the school next door.'

'Yes, I am now,' said Sara. 'But I wasn't at first.'

The Indian gentleman looked at Mr Carmichael, and then Mr Carmichael looked at Sara.

'What do you mean by "at first", child?' he asked.

'When Father first took me to the school.'

'Where is your father?' said Mr Carmichael.

'He died,' said Sara, very quietly. 'His friend ran away with all his money, and there wasn't any money for me. There was nobody to take care of me. So Miss Minchin put me in the attic and said I must work for my bread.'

true what really
happens or
happened

The Indian gentleman looked at Sara. 'What — what was your father's name?' he said. 'Tell me.'

Sara looked at him sadly. 'Ralph Crewe,' she said. 'He died in India from a fever, two years ago.'

Mr Carrisford's face went very white. 'Carmichael,' he whispered, 'it is the child — the child!'

*   *   *

That was an exciting day for many people. At first poor Sara did not understand. But Mr Carmichael talked to her quietly and told her everything — the true story about her father's friend and the diamond mines, and the two years of looking for Ralph Crewe's daughter.

'And all the time,' she said later to Mr Carrisford, when they sat by his fire, 'I was in the house next door.'

'Yes,' he said. 'And you're never going back there. Your home is with me now. I'm going to take care of Ralph's Little Missus.'

Sara laughed happily. 'And you were the friend, too. All those beautiful things in my attic came from you – you and Ram Dass.'

The Indian gentleman smiled at her. 'We were sorry for you,' he said. 'Ram Dass can move very quietly, and he carried the things across the roof when you were out. I couldn't find Ralph's daughter, but I wanted to help somebody. And then Ram Dass told me about this sad little servant-girl in the attic next door.'

And so the story ended happily for everybody – but not for Miss Minchin. Sara was very rich now and Miss Minchin wanted her to come back to the school. She came to see Mr Carrisford, but he said some very angry things to her and she went away with a red face.

Becky came to live in Mr Carrisford's house, too. She was Sara's servant, and she was very happy. She had a warm room, nice dresses and good things to eat every day. And she loved Sara very much.

Ermengarde often came to visit Sara, and Sara helped her with her school lessons again. Ermengarde was not clever, but she was a true friend. On that first day in the Indian gentleman's house, Sara wrote a letter to her, and Ermengarde carried the letter into the schoolroom.

'There *were* diamond mines,' she told Lavinia and the other girls. 'There *were*! There were millions and millions of diamonds in the mines, and half of them are Sara's. And they were her diamonds all the time when she was cold and hungry in the attic. And she was a princess *then*, and she's a princess *now*!'

true friend a friend who is always a good friend

Activities

1 Complete the sentences with the words.

wrong   millions   friend   happily   true   ~~Russia~~

1 Mr Carmichael went to _____*Russia*_____ to look for Sara.

2 He found Emily Carew, who was the _____ girl.

3 Mr Carmichael told Sara the _____ story about what happened.

4 There were _____ of diamonds in the mines.

5 The story did not end _____ for Miss Minchin.

6 Ermengarde was not clever, but she was a true _____ .

2 What did you think about the people in this story? Choose the names and finish these sentences in your own words.

Sara   Ermengarde   Lavinia   Becky   Mr Crewe   Ram Dass

Miss Minchin   Mr Carrisford

1 I was sorry for _____ because _____
_____

2 I liked _____ because _____
_____

3 I didn't like _____ because _____
_____

4 _____ was right to _____
_____

5 _____ was wrong to _____
_____

3 Here is a new illustration for the story. Find the best place in the story to put the picture, and answer these questions.

The picture goes on page _____.

1 Who is Sara talking to? _____

2 What is happening in Sara's room at this moment? _____

_____

3 What happens next? _____

_____

Now write a title for the illustration.

Title: _____

Project

1 **At the end of the story Sara wrote a letter to Ermengarde. Complete her letter with the words below. Use one word for each gap.**

after better care diamonds fever find friend Half house

kind know live mines next nicest servant ~~wonderful~~

Dear Ermie,
    I have something _wonderful_ to tell you! I am writing
this in the Indian gentleman's _____. His name is
Mr Carrisford, and he was my father's _____ in India.
And, Ermie, there WERE _____ in the _____ –
millions of them – but they only found them _____
my father died.
    Mr Carrisford was ill with a _____ too, and when
he got _____, he came to England to look for me. But
he couldn't _____ me because he didn't _____
my name. And all the time, Ermie, I was a _____ in
the house _____ door! _____ of the diamonds
are mine now, Mr Carrisford says. But the _____
thing is this, Ermie. Mr Carrisford is a very _____ man,
and he wants to take _____ of me. So I'm going to
_____ with him and have a home again. You must
come and visit me soon.
    Your best friend,
    Sara

2 **Here's Ermengarde's reply to Sara's letter. Put the words in the correct order.**

Dear Sara,

you / . / Thank / for / letter / your

Thank you for your letter.

home / a / happy / I'm / you / have / . / now / that

_____

. / you / kind / to / that / Mr Carrisford / I'm / glad / is

_____

rich / Lavinia / that / is / cross / are / you / .

_____

friends / can / hope / . / still / I / be / we / that

_____

soon / I / visit / you / want / . / to

_____

Your best friend,

Ermie

OXFORD
UNIVERSITY PRESS

Great Clarendon Street, Oxford OX2 6DP

Oxford University Press is a department of the University of Oxford.
It furthers the University's objective of excellence in research, scholarship,
and education by publishing worldwide in

Oxford New York

Auckland Cape Town Dar es Salaam Hong Kong Karachi
Kuala Lumpur Madrid Melbourne Mexico City Nairobi
New Delhi Shanghai Taipei Toronto

With offices in

Argentina Austria Brazil Chile Czech Republic France Greece
Guatemala Hungary Italy Japan Poland Portugal Singapore
South Korea Switzerland Thailand Turkey Ukraine Vietnam

OXFORD and OXFORD ENGLISH are registered trade marks of
Oxford University Press in the UK and in certain other countries

ISBN: 978 0 19 480269 7

Printed in China

ACKNOWLEDGEMENTS
Illustrations by: Bob Doucet/Bright Agency

What Holidays
Do You Have?

Written by Josephine Selwyn

Celebrations

Vital Vocabulary

I am North American.
I have a holiday for Thanksgiving.
I have turkey.
I like turkey.

North-American boy

turkey

This turkey is my Thanksgiving dinner.

I am Australian.
I have a holiday for Christmas.
I have a Christmas tree.
I give presents.

Australian boy

presents

We have lots of presents under our Christmas tree.

I am Chinese.
I have a holiday for New Year.
I see dragons.
I give presents.

Chinese boy

dragon

I see dragons like this at the New Year parade.

9

I am English.
I have a holiday for Easter.
I have Easter eggs.
I like Easter eggs.

English girl

I am Indian.
I have a holiday for Diwali.
I light candles.
I give presents.

Indian girl

candle

We light lots of candles for Diwali.

We like our holidays.
Our friends like our holidays, too.

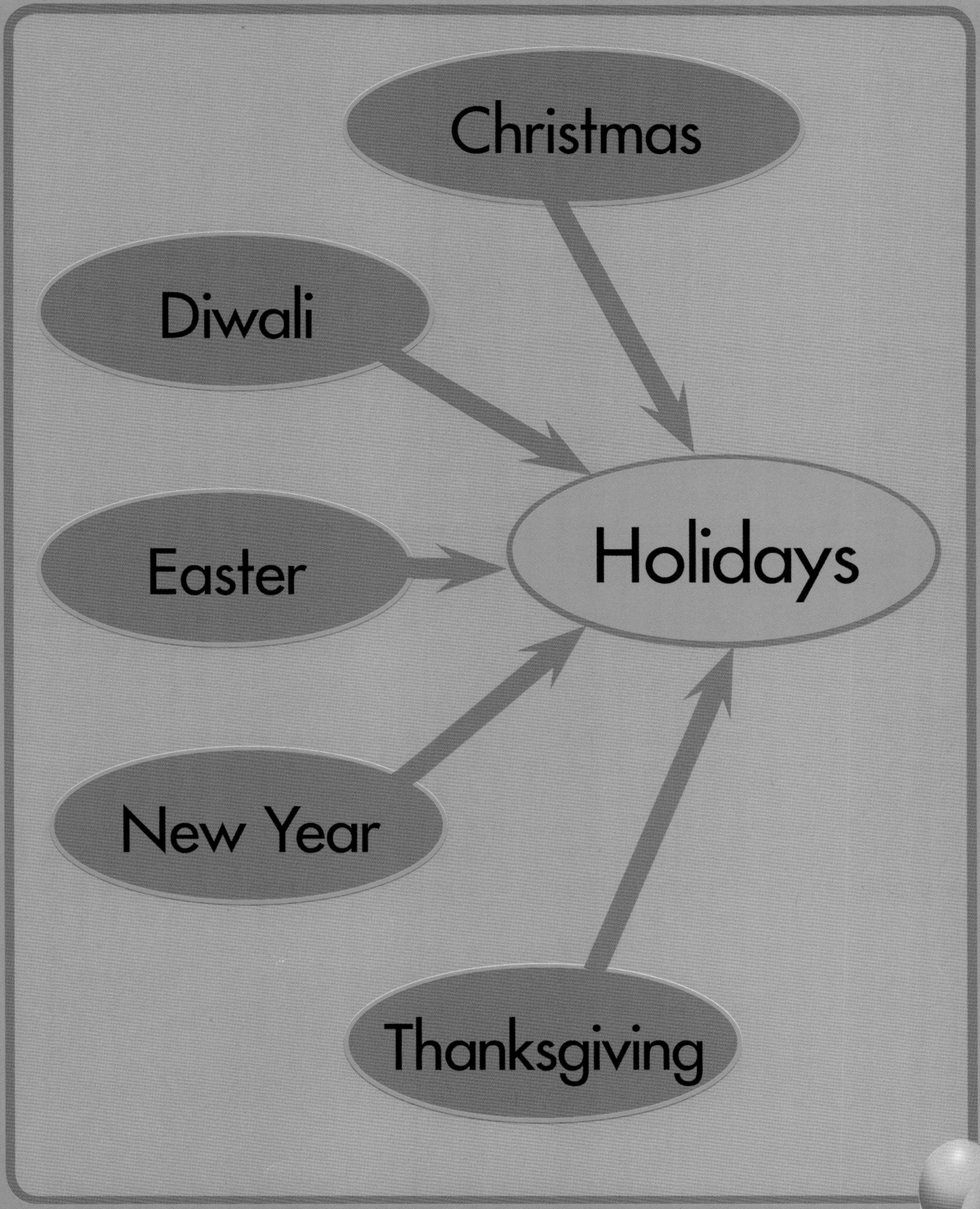

Christmas

Diwali

Easter

Holidays

New Year

Thanksgiving

Critical Thinking

These are fireworks.
Find out which holidays
have fireworks.